PRE

John Moschus was a monk from
situated in the neighbourhood
taking with him his young p
later to become Patriarch of Jer
the Christian world as he kr
included modern North Africa, Egypt, r ai....

He set out not to sell anything, or to preach the latest
brand of orthodoxy, but to gather evidence to support his
underlying conviction that heroic deeds and unselfish
sacrifice were not all that uncommon in this world, and were
not to be found exclusively in the great and the famous. He
thought that such spiritual treasures could be found in
abundance in the lives of ordinary men and women of all
nations, all classes, and all occupations. This evidence he
collated into the collection of stories he called *The Spiritual
Meadow*. He believed that if you only opened your eyes and
looked around you would find yourself in the midst of a
spiritual meadow where there were wild flowers of every
shade, endowed with the greatest variety of perfumes, and
colours, and growing in profusion, though often unnoticed by
those rushing down the highways. He undertook his tour like
some promiscuous bee, moving through this spiritual meadow
and gathering sweet nectar from any blossom he found.

His collection method was simplicity itself. He found and
interviewed anyone who had a good story to tell. It was not
necessarily a highly moral story; it only needed to catch your
eye and hold your attention. On this principle he gathered
his nectar not just from hermits, anchorites, and pillar saints:
he also took evidence from sailors, prostitutes, gangsters, and
even animals, and by this method he left us with a unique
record of the life lived at street level by ordinary folk in the
last years of the great Justinian's empire. No one else took the
time to note down the ephemeral stories of these humble
people and to record their conversations for posterity as this
man did. He was not interested in theological disputations,

dynastic manipulations or philosophical speculations. He recorded the events that overtook the ordinary men and women of his day, their unhappy defeats in life and their frequent victories against all the odds.

There is an added poignancy for us in John Moschus' work, of which he was completely unaware. Even as he and Sophronius tramped those dusty roads and interviewed countless ordinary people, across the desert in far-off Mecca the prophet Mohamed was growing to maturity. In due course he would unleash amongst his compatriots a storm of zeal for their newly-found faith that would almost completely sweep away the Christian culture in all those centres where John Moschus was gathering his evidence. His intimate record, then, is of the last generation of Christians before the flood-waters of Islam inundated so many of them. In modern terms we would describe *The Spiritual Meadow* as a rare and valuable piece of investigative journalism.

The accounts in this book are compiled in the form of a *florilegium*, an anthology, taken from the complete text as found in J.-P. Migne, *Patrologia Graeca*, 87: 2851-3116. They are collected together under headings which illustrate several themes found in the original text. The numbers after the titles of the stories refer to their place in Migne's manuscript.

But why delay any further? Let John speak for himself in the words he used to dedicate his work to his friend and companion on his travels, Sophronius.

Ralph Martin SSM
December 2012

On Tour in Byzantium

Excerpts from
The Spiritual Meadow
of
John Moschus

Translated by Ralph Martin SSM

SLG Press
Convent of the Incarnation Fairacres
Parker Street Oxford OX4 1TB England
www.slgpress.co.uk

First published by SLG Press 2013

© Translation by Ralph Martin SSM, 2013

© Cover image, Jim Forest

ISBN: 978-0-7283-0240-2
ISSN: 0307-1405

Printed by Joshua Horgan, Oxford

The Spiritual Meadow

PROLOGUE

The meadows in the springtime, my friend, give me immense pleasure with the sight of an infinite variety of blossoms. The view brings the passer-by to a halt and regales him with many shades of delight and colour. The eyes are dazzled by the variety of blossoms and the senses are soothed by their perfumes. This corner of the meadow is glowing with the scarlet of roses, and another corner is filled with lilies which gently draw the eye from the roses towards themselves. In yet another spot the violets are in bloom, clad in the purple of emperors, in fact. The flowers in their untold numbers pour forth all around us rich gifts of pleasure and delight.

Understand then, Sophronius, faithful and devout son that you are, that this is exactly what this present work is: a springtime meadow. You will find in these pages the noble deeds of those men and women who are the lights of our own generation. They are those who, as the psalmist says, are planted by the waterside and all of them, by the gift of Christ our God, are the friends of God. Each one is different, each is adorned with his own particular beauty, grace, and courage, and from this meadow of life I have selected some fair blossoms and woven them into a crown to offer to you, my faithful son, and through you to everyone.

That is why I have called this present work *The Spiritual Meadow*, because it too can bring gladness of heart and refreshment of soul to all who come across it. For nobility and dedication of life are not to be found only through long meditations on holy topics or thinking holy thoughts and all that sort of thing. No! They are also to be found in the lives of all kinds of people such as I have here recorded. That is why I took up this task, my son; I wanted to build up your love and make it grow. I have been like the very wisest of bees drawing nectar from every sort of blossom for your edification.

ANIMAL STORIES

Like many holy women and men through the ages, John Moschus seems to have had a natural affinity with the wild beasts. He even collected a story of one man's pet lion, a story he tells in some detail:

Jordan the Lion (107)

About a mile from the banks of the sacred Jordan river stands a monastery named for the holy father Gerasimus. When we visited this monastery, the inmates there told us this story about that saintly man:

One day as that holy man Gerasimus was walking along the edges of the sacred Jordan, he came across a lion roaring with pain because of his foot. His foot was pierced with a thorn from one of the shrubs and was now swollen and full of pus. As soon as the lion caught sight of our father, he ran towards him and displayed the stricken paw with the thorn still imbedded in it. In his dumb way, he was suffering greatly, and, as it were, asking what help or healing our father could provide for him.

When our old father saw the beast in such a sorry state, he sat down, lifted up the paw into his lap, and pulled out the thorn, and along with it came a discharge of putrid matter. He then thoroughly cleansed the wound, bound up the paw with a linen bandage, and let him go.

But the lion, once healed, refused to part with our old father and followed him about like a most promising novice. Our father was filled with admiration to see such nobility of soul in a brute beast, and from that day on he fed him, setting out for him bits of bread and some cooked lentils.

The monastery drew its water from the Jordan, and since the river was a mile off, they had a donkey who worked for the monks. The brothers gradually adopted the custom of putting the lion in charge of the donkey when it was grazing along the riverside. However, one day the donkey strayed a little too far away from the lion so that when some Arab traders came by on camels and found the donkey alone, they took it captive and led it off in their train.

The lion returned to Father Gerasimus at the monastery with his eyes downcast and with sullen glances. Our father immediately assumed that the lion had eaten the donkey and asked him, 'Where is our donkey?' But he, like a man accused, stood silent gazing at his feet.

Again our old man spoke, 'Bless my soul! You have eaten him. Well then, from now on you must undertake all the donkey's chores.'

So from that day, whenever the father called him, the lion would take up his pack-saddle with its four great jars and go off to fetch water. There came a day when a soldier came to the monastery to pray with our father, and when he saw the lion carrying the water jars, and heard the story behind it, he felt sorry for him. Out of his purse he drew three coins, which he gave to the brothers so that they might buy a donkey for the water duty and set the lion free from these social services.

Some time after the lion had been freed from his duties, the camel drivers who had stolen the first donkey happened again to pass along that way to sell wheat in the holy city, still having that donkey in their train. As they were crossing through the Jordan, the lion and the donkey by chance met again. As soon as he saw him, the donkey deserted his camels and escaped, while the lion, immediately recognizing his donkey, ran up to him and began nibbling the donkey's bridle with his teeth as he always used to do.

He then pulled him away, along with the three camels, fairly roaring with joy and bliss, for that donkey which had been lost was now found. He brought them all to our father who all along had been assuming that the lion had eaten the donkey. At last he realized that the lion had been falsely accused, and in compensation, from that time on, he gave him the name Jordan. The lion stayed in the monastery with our father for fifteen years, and in all that time he was never far from his side.

The day came when Father Gerasimus departed to be with the Lord and was buried by the brothers. But in the providence of God, it happened that on that day the lion was absent from the monastery. Shortly thereafter the lion returned and began looking for our father. Father Sabbatios explained to him that our father had gone to be with the Lord, but Jordan made it clear that he would in no way accept such bereavement. Sabbatios and the rest of the brothers, seeing his distress, gathered around him, rubbing his back and counselling him. But his howling continued to increase, and increase again, as he augmented his mourning with still more vociferous wails and roars. In this way, not only vocally but with his countenance, with his eyes, he made clear to all the enormous grief he felt at no longer seeing our father.

Then Father Sabbatios said to him, 'Since you refuse to believe us, come with me and I will show you the place where we have laid our father.' So he took him along and led him to the place where the grave was, about half a mile from the church.

Then Father Sabbatios, standing by the grave of Father Gerasimus, said to the lion, 'Look! Here is our father.' And he knelt down and prayed.

When the lion saw how he was kneeling there, he beat his own head against the ground and suddenly, with a mighty roar, he breathed his last and fell across our father's grave.

All these things happened not because the lion had a soul or was imbued with reason, but because it is God's way to give the glory to those who give the glory to him, not just in their lifetime but also after their death; and it was also to show what sort of relationship existed between the wild beasts and Adam before he disobeyed God's command and was exiled from Paradise.

Then there is the tale of the vegetarian lion:

The Vegetarian Lion (163)

The father Alexander from the Calamon monastery, hard by the Jordan, told us this tale:

One day, when I was in the hermitage of the father Paul, the Greek, someone came and knocked on the door, and the old father went out and opened it to him. He then fetched out a dish of soaked bread and lentils and put it down for someone to eat. I assumed that this person was a traveller who had come by, but when I looked out the window I saw that it was a lion.

So I said to the father, 'Holy father, why are you feeding this lion?'

And he explained, 'I urged him that if he would do no more harm to man or beast, then he could come here each day and I would give him his food. And now, look, for the past seven months he has come to me twice a day, and I have been providing him with his meals.'

A few days later I was at his place again, hoping to buy a flask of wine from him, and I greeted him, 'How is it with you today, holy father? How is your lion friend doing?'

But he answered, 'He's doing very badly, very badly.'

So I said, 'What's all this about?'

And he told me, 'He came here yesterday, expecting me to give him something to eat, but I noticed that his chin was all flecked with blood, so I demanded, "What's the meaning of this? You have disobeyed me and you have been eating flesh. Bless my soul if I ever again give you any share in the brothers' food. Get away from here, you carnivore." But he was reluctant to leave until I took a rope of three strands and gave him three hearty strokes. Then he left.'

And the case of the lion who refused to be a martyr-maker:

The Failed Martyr (101)

The brothers of the same monastery also told us about another old father of theirs. This old man died a few years ago. His name was Paul, and he came from a Roman family.

One day he went off to the city with his mules. But while resting at an inn along the way, the machinations of Satan caused one of the father's mules, all unbeknownst to him, to tread on a little child and so kill him.

So grief-stricken was Paul by this accident that he withdrew from the monastery altogether. He went up into the Arona country and became a hermit. There he grieved unceasingly over the death of that little child, and would repeat over and over again, 'I am the murderer of that little child, and as a murderer I will be judged.' Now there was a lion in that neighbourhood, and each day the father would visit the lion's den to poke him with a stick so that he would rise up in anger and devour him. But the lion refused to harm him in any way whatsoever.

Then when Paul saw that he was not getting anywhere, he said to himself, 'I will go and sleep in the lion's path so that when he gets up to go down to the river to drink water, he will gobble me up.'

So he laid himself down, but when, in a little while, the lion came that way, he stepped over the old man with an almost human dignity and poise. He refused even to touch him.

Then the old man was thus fully assured that God had forgiven him his sin, and he went back to the monastery. There he led a life that was a blessing and an inspiration to his brothers, until the day when he laid down to rest in God.

Another lion was remembered chiefly for his courtesy:

The Courteous Lion (181)

Father Dionysius told us another tale about this same anchorite:

It seems that the old man was walking one day in the region around the village of Sachus, near where his cave was, and as he walked he saw a huge lion coming towards him and getting very near. The road was very narrow at that point; it ran between two fields. The farmers there are accustomed to protect their fields by planting a hedge of thorn bushes all around them. This makes the path so narrow that even a solitary man without baggage could scarcely get through and continue on his way without hindrance.

Now, as the old man and the lion drew closer to one another, the old man would not turn aside to give way to the lion, nor would the lion turn aside to give way to the man; but it was impossible for them to pass each other as the path was far too narrow. However, when the lion saw that this servant of God intended to come straight on and had no thought of giving way, he stood up on his hind legs and leaned against the thorn bushes on the old man's left side. And pushing with all his weight and physical strength he managed to make the path a little wider so that the righteous man could continue his journey unhindered and so he did, brushing past the lion's backside. When he had passed the lion allowed the bushes to spring back and he, too, continued on his way.

Perhaps we can conclude this section with a story of one of the first 'Friends of the Earth':

The Animal Lover (184)

When we were in the ninth district at Alexandria, we put up at the monastery of Father John the Eunuch for some spiritual refreshment. There we met a very old man who had been in the monastery about eighty years This man was kinder and more merciful than any man we have ever met, not just to human beings but to the whole animal creation. Works of love made up the totality of the old man's occupations. Getting up early, well before dawn, he put out food for every dog in the monastery, then he put out some flour for the littlest ants, and some grain for the bigger ones. After this he soaked some biscuits and scattered them over the roofs so that the birds might have something to eat. During the whole time that he lived in the monastery he had no use for doors or windows or mirrors or candles or plates. To make a long story short, he had no use for any of the things of this world. He never owned—even for one hour—any cash or any book or even a shirt; instead he handed over anything he ever had to those in need. He had another world in view.

MARRIAGE

In an age when most monks looked on marriage with a jaundiced eye, and all forms of connubial bliss as a snare of the devil, John Moschus records several stories of husbands and wives who were devoted to each other. By their faithfulness to one another and by their Christian faith they overcame apparently insurmountable obstacles, eventually to discover a rich reward.

The Moneylenders (185)

While we were on the island of Samos, Mary, the mother of Paul, the mayor, who is a great worker amongst the poor, told us this tale:

When I was in the city of Nisibis I met a woman who was a Christian, though her husband was still a traditional believer. Between them they had fifty pounds. One day the man said to his wife, 'Let's loan our money out so that our profits will multiply. If we spend it one pound at a time we will soon have used up the lot.'

And his wife in reply said, 'If you are minded to loan the money out, why not loan it to the God of the Christians?'

So he said, 'And where is this God of the Christians, so we can make him a loan?'

'I will show him to you,' she answered, 'and not only will you not lose your money but he will pay you interest on it so as to double your capital.'

'Let's go,' said he, 'show me where he is and we can make him a loan.'

At once she took her husband and led him to the cathedral in Nisibis which has five great gates before it. She brought him into the church's portico within the gates and pointed out to him the poor beggars sitting about there, and said, 'If you give your money to these folk, the God of the Christians will accept it, for all of these are his people.'

9

The man was happy enough to divide up his fifty pounds amongst these beggars, and then they both went home.

Three months later when they were now completely unable to pay any of their bills, the man asked his wife, 'Now, my dear, we are broke, so is it not time for the God of the Christians to pay back that loan?'

'Certainly,' she said, 'go to the place where you made the loan and he will repay—no problem.'

The man set off on the run and came to the cathedral. But when he went inside, to the very place where he had divided his money amongst the beggars, he expected to see someone who would hand back the money to him. But even though he walked through the whole church, he saw no one except the same beggars sitting in the same places. He stood there, racking his brain for what he could say or to whom he could say it, when he saw, lying on the marble floor right at his feet, one pound, all that was left of all those he had shared with his poor brothers and sisters. Bending down, he scooped it up and returned home to his partner.

'Look,' he said, 'I went to that church of yours and, believe me, woman, I saw never a sign of that God of the Christians you are always going on about. I got nothing except, perhaps, this one pound which I found lying there on the spot where I gave away the fifty.'

But that remarkable woman, never at a loss for words, replied, 'Don't you see? He is invisible; by invisible power with an invisible arm, he manages this whole universe. So off you go, father dear; buy us something for our supper today, and he will surely provide something for us for tomorrow.'

Off he went and bought some bread, some wine, and a fish, and gave them to his wife to prepare. She took the fish and began to clean it, but when she cut it open she found in the stomach a marvellous-looking stone. The woman was greatly amazed and, although she had no idea what it was, she knew enough to hold on to it.

When her husband came in and they were eating their supper, she showed him the stone she had found. 'Look,' she said, 'this is the stone I found in the fish.'

When he saw it he too was amazed, but neither did he have any idea what kind of stone it was. When supper was over he said to her, 'Give the stone to me and I will go and sell it if I can find anyone who might take it.' As I said, he was an illiterate man of very limited experience and so he never realized what he had got in his hand. Putting the stone in his pocket, he went off to the merchant who deals in precious stones. He arrived to find the man shutting up his shop, for by this time it was getting dark.

He began this way, 'Would you be interested in buying this little stone?'

The dealer took a look and replied, 'How much are you asking for it?'

And the man replied, 'Make me an offer.'

And then the merchant, 'I'll give you five pounds for it.'

The man, thinking the merchant was trying to make a fool of him said, 'What? Five pounds for this?'

The merchant, thinking the man was being devious with his ambiguous answer said, 'I'll give you ten pounds.'

But the man, still thinking that he was being made a fool of, said nothing, and the dealer added, 'I'll make it twenty.'

But the man still kept silent, answering never a word. The dealer went up to thirty, then to fifty, and swore an oath that he could in fact pay that price. As it went on, the man began to realize that unless the stone were truly valuable, the merchant would not be willing to make such offers. Little by little the merchant raised the price until he came to three hundred pounds, at which point the man accepted the offer, surrendered the stone, and went home to his wife very, very happy.

When she saw him she asked, 'How much did you get?' thinking maybe he had sold it for fifty or sixty pence.

But he handed over to her the three hundred pounds. 'That's how much I got for it!'

Filled with amazement at the generosity and kindness of God, she said, 'Now you can see, my dear man, how good, how beautiful, how generous the God of the Christians is. Notice this: He has not only given you back the fifty pounds that you loaned him, but with interest as well, calculated at six times the original, after only a few months. Now can't you see that there is no other God in all the world or in all the heavens? He is the only one.'

Fully persuaded by this miracle, and having learned the truth from his own experience, the man became a Christian without delay and gave the glory to God our Christ and Saviour with the Father and the Holy Spirit. Also, again and again, he gave thanks for the wisdom of his dear wife through whom it was granted to him to know the true God.

And here is another example of a virtuous couple who reap their due reward:

The Loyal Wife (189)

At Ascalon we stayed at the inn of the fathers, and while we were there, Father Eusebius the priest told us this tale:

There was a trader in our town who lost everything he had in a shipwreck, along with everything else others had invested with him. He was the only survivor. When he arrived back here, he was arrested by his creditors who seized every bit of property he had and threw him into prison. There was not a single thing left to him except the clothes he had on his back and those of his wife. In such a tight corner, when both were overwhelmed with despair, the wife tried at least to provide some bread to feed her husband, as he requested.

One day she was sitting in the prison taking a meal with her husband when one of the town's big philanthropists came in to distribute his charity money to some of the inmates there. As soon as he saw this woman—who was not one of the prisoners—sitting at her husband's side, he was pierced to the heart, for she was exceptionally beautiful. He summoned her through one of the guards and she came up to him gladly, naturally expecting to receive some kind of donation.

He took her to one side, and in private asked her, 'What's your problem? Why are you here?' And she soon told him the whole story.

Then he said, 'If I pay the whole debt you owe, will you sleep with me tonight?'

But this woman was not just a beauty; she had a lot of intelligence. So she answered, 'Well, my master, I have heard the great apostle say that the wife does not have authority over her own body; it is the husband who carries that authority. So, my master, give me a few minutes to consult my husband, and whatever he tells me to do I will do.'

So then she went and told the whole business to her husband. The husband, who was a shrewd man, and full of affection for his wife, was not swept off his feet by the chance of escaping from prison. Instead, with a heavy sigh and even with tears in his eyes, he told his wife, 'Dear sister, go and send that man packing; instead, let us place our hopes in God. He will not let us down in the end.'

So she got up and sent the man away with the words, 'I spoke to my husband and he won't agree.'

It happened that there was at the same time a local gangster incarcerated in the inner prison from where he was able to observe the whole affair of the man and his wife. As he did so he gave a great sigh of grief and said to himself, 'Look now at what a mess this pair has got themselves into, and yet they did not put their integrity up for sale in order to get hold of some money and gain their freedom. They reckoned self-respect to be worth more than all the money in the world, and they despised the usual values of modern life. Yet here in the same place is a miserable bastard like me who has never had a single thought in his head about whether God even exists or not, and, no doubt as a consequence of that, I have been guilty of so many murders.'

Then he beckoned the couple over to the little window of the cell where he had been locked up, and said, 'I have long been a gangster and am guilty of so many crimes and murders. I know for sure that as soon as the governor appears in this town, I will be led outside for execution as a murderer. I was deeply moved when I saw how you two have conducted yourselves so honestly. Now, if you go to this particular spot in the city wall and dig there, whatever money you find will be yours. Use it to pay all your debts. Don't worry; there will be plenty left over. Pray for me that I also may find mercy.'

A few days later the governor arrived in town, and he ordered the gangster to be taken out and beheaded. The next day the wife asked her husband, 'My husband, will you now be advising me to go to the spot the gangster told us of and see if he was telling the truth?'

And he replied, 'Do whatever you think is best.'

When evening came, she took a small trowel and went to the place and dug. There she found a covered earthenware pot, full of gold. The way she dealt with the money was very sensible. She paid it out little by little, now to this creditor and now to that one until all had been repaid and she was able to bring her husband out of prison.

The one who told us this tale drew this lesson from it: 'This pair kept the commandments of God. See then how the Lord our God multiplied his mercies upon them'

HUMOUR

Humour is a rather rare commodity in the world of the Desert Fathers and a person may search hard and long to find anything resembling what we would call 'a joke.' But how else are we to comprehend the following story, except as 'a joke'?

Respite in Hell (44)

When we arrived in Thebes, one of the fathers there told us that outside the city of Antinous there was an outstanding hermit who had spent about seventy years in that cell.

He had ten novices, but one of them was far from zealous about matters spiritual. Many a time did the old father warn and exhort him, 'My dear brother, take some thought for your soul, for you too must die, and then you will surely find yourself in a place of punishment.'

However, the brother paid no heed whatsoever. He never believed a word the old man said. So it happened that after a while the brother did die and the old father grieved deeply for him, because he was only too aware that he had departed this world in a callous and careless spirit. He then began to pray, 'Lord Jesus Christ, our true God, show me what has happened to the soul of this our brother.'

He was then caught up in a vision and he saw a river of fire with multitudes standing in the flames; and there in the midst of them, with the flames licking around his throat, was that brother.

Then the old man said, 'Didn't I warn you time and again about this very punishment so that you would be serious about your soul?'

But this was the brother's reply. 'My father, I can, even now, still give thanks to God; at least my head has some relief from the flames. You see father, because of your prayers I am standing on the head of a bishop!'

MONKS AND HERMITS

Of course, one of the main interests for John is in those people who inhabit the monasteries, hermitages, and even the pillars, around the eastern end of the Mediterranean. He records one or two instances of what in our day we would call a 'late vocation'—a person of mature years well-established in their way of life, who find themselves deeply drawn to a religious vocation. The first example is particularly striking, dealing as it does with a man who is a successful gangster.

The Late Vocation (143)

When we arrived at Antinous in Thebes, we went to see Philamon, a very learned man there, in order to confer with him. This is what he told us.

There was a certain gangster, David by name, in the region of Hermapolis. This man stripped many of their property, and many of their lives; in short, he committed a greater variety of crimes than any other I have ever heard of, if I may say so.

However, one day while he was still living in the hills with more than thirty of his men around him, all still in the midst of their thievery, he suddenly came to his senses and was filled with remorse for all the crimes he had committed.

At once he said goodbye to his band, and went to a monastery where he knocked at the door. The door-keeper came out to him, and asked, 'What do you want?'

To which the head gangster replied, 'I want to be a monk.'

So the doorkeeper went inside and reported the whole story to the abbot, who came out at once. But when he saw that this man was middle-aged, he refused him. 'No, you cannot stay here; you would never stand up to our monastic rule of life. The life of a brother here is a very, very hard life under an extremely strict discipline, and that has not been your way hitherto.'

But the man pleaded, 'No! I can do it. Only give me a chance.'

But the abbot stood firm, 'You could never do it.'

Then the head gangster began to speak very seriously to him, 'I would like you to be aware that I am David, the head of this local gang, and the reason why I wanted to come here was to make reparation for my many crimes. But if you persist in refusing me admittance, rest fully assured—for this I swear by him whose home is in the heavens—that I will return to my former occupations and friends. Next, I will come back here with all my colleagues and we will put the lot of you to death and pull your little monastery to pieces.'

Without further ado, the abbot welcomed him into the monastery, gave him the tonsure, and clothed him in the holy habit. Then did the man begin to compete seriously in the spiritual combat. In his fasting, his obedience, his humility, he surpassed all the other brothers. There were about seventy brothers in the monastery, but David was such a blessing to each one that he became a role model for all.

One day, while he was sitting in his cell, the angel of the Lord appeared, calling him, 'David! David! The Lord has now forgiven all your offences, and from now on you will be a miracle-worker.'

But he answered the angel in this way, 'I find it hard to believe that in so short a time the Lord God has forgiven all those many grievous offences of mine, which still seem heavier to me than the sand along the seashore.'

Then the angel said, 'When Zachariah the priest refused to believe me when I promised him a son, I did not treat it lightly. I bound his tongue to show him the results of disbelieving any word spoken by me. So, is it likely that I shall now spare you? From now on you will remain totally dumb.'

Then David bowed low before the angel, saying, 'When I was in the world breaking every law and shedding innocent blood, I talked with abandon all the day. So why is it now, when my only wish is to serve God and to sing his praises with psalms and hymns, that you bind my tongue and make me dumb?'

'Very well,' replied the angel, 'You will be able to speak as long as you are singing the services in the choir. Outside service times you will remain totally dumb.'

And that is exactly what happened. God worked many a miracle through him. He was able to sing all the psalms in choir, but apart from the psalms he could not utter a word, great or small.

The one who told us this testified, 'I often used to see him and I used to give God the glory because of him.'

But it was not only gangsters; prostitutes also often felt a call to religious life, as in this case:

The Wise Prostitute (31)

Two of the brothers were travelling from Aegis to Tarsus in Cilicia, when, in the providence of God, they came to a certain inn where they decided to take some rest, for they were travelling in high summer.

They found there three young men on their way to Aegis who had brought a prostitute along with them. The brothers sat down in a spot by themselves, and one of them pulled out of his bag a copy of the gospels, which he began to read. When the prostitute who was accompanying the young men noticed the brother reading, she got up from the young men and went and sat down beside the brother.

He, in an attempt to shake her off, said, 'What a shameless hussy you must be. Don't you blush to come over so boldly to sit here with us?'

But she replied, 'Don't loathe me so, father. Even if I am full of all manner of sin, yet the Lord and Master of us all, our very God, never turned away the prostitute that approached him.'

Then the brother said, 'Yes, but that prostitute gave up her prostitution.'

And she said, 'Yes indeed, and, placing all my hope on the Son of the Living God, it is my intention from this day forward to forsake this sin forever.'

And on that day she left the young men and all her possessions behind, and followed after the two brothers.

They found her a place in a monastery near to Aegis that went by the name of the Shearer's. I myself met this woman there in her old age, a woman of great understanding. That was when she told me this whole story.

Her name was Maria.

Not only prostitutes, but comedians from the stage felt the same call:

Comedian to Hermit (32)

There was a certain comedian in Tarsus in Cilicia by the name of Babylas. He lived there with two concubines, Komitas and Nicola, and with them he lived the high life, doing anything whatsoever his demons put into his head to do.

One day he went into a church where the gospel was being read, and, by the providence of God, it happened to be that passage that says, 'Repent for the kingdom of heaven is at hand.'

He was pricked to the heart by these words and began with tears to lament his condition and all his previous habits. The minute he came out of church he went home and called his concubines.

'You well know the manner in which I have lived the high life with you, but I have never shown any favoritism to one or the other of you. So! Look now! All my possessions are yours, take everything I have and divide it up between you. From this day forward I am going to renounce the world in order to become a monk.'

The two women, with one voice and with many tears, responded, 'We have been your partners in sin to the ruin of our lives, and now when you plan to undertake a work so well-pleasing to God, do you want to leave us behind and do it all on your own? Never! We won't allow it. Instead we will become your partners in the good life.'

The comedian straightway had himself enclosed as a hermit within one of the towers in the city wall. The two women sold up all his possessions and gave away the proceeds to the poor and put on the monastic habit. They had a cell prepared by the city wall and enclosed themselves as hermits also.

I met this man, and very beneficial the meeting was to me. He was the humblest of men, totally understanding, totally accepting.

I wrote up this account of his life for the building-up of my readers.

But, in spite of the widest possible variation in styles and manners of living, the monks retained a very clear idea of what constituted the true religious:

The True Monk (24)

The elders who lived in the lavra at Chouziba told us this tale about one of their brothers:

When this man was still living in his village, he already had this fixed habit that whenever he saw anyone in the village so poverty-stricken that he didn't have the wherewithal to sow his own fields, he would go by night, taking his own seed and his own oxen with him, and sow the neighbour's field without the owner of that field knowing anything about it.

Later, when this brother came out into the desert and fetched up at our lavra at Chouziba, he still exercised the same sort of compassion. He used to travel up and down the road that leads from the Jordan River to the holy city of Jerusalem, and he always carried with him extra bread and water. If he found anyone staggering under a heavy load, he would carry his burden for him, and he would be ready to carry it as far as the holy Mount of Olives; and, if he found others in the same fix on the way back, he would carry their loads also, even as far as Jericho.

That's how you would see the old man, sometimes sweating under a great heavy load, sometimes carrying a child on his shoulder, at times even two children. At other times you would see him sitting at the roadside mending the broken sandal of some man or woman, for he carried with him all he needed for that job.

To some he would give a drink from the water he carried, and with others he shared his bread. If he saw someone nearly naked, he would strip off his own shirt and give it to him. And if he came across a dead body in the road, he would sing the requiem office over him and then bury him.

You would find him any day of the week, toiling up and down that road.

However, it would seem that the hermit's cell was by no means his castle; rather, the door stood open and he was available and accessible to every passer-by:

Temptations (136)

Father John, who was a priest at the monastery of the Eunuchs, heard this tale from Sisinus, a hermit, who told him:

21

One day as I was in my cave near the holy river Jordan singing the psalms appointed for 9:00 in the morning, a Saracen woman came and walked right into my cave.

She came and stood in front of me and stripped herself naked. While remaining calm, I continued singing my psalms without alarm and in the praise of God.

When I had finished, I said to her in the Hebrew tongue, 'Sit down while I have some talk with you, and after that I will do whatever you like.'

She sat down, and I went on, 'Are you a Christian or a traditional believer?'

She answered, 'I am a Christian.'

So then I asked her, 'And don't you know where prostitutes finish up?'

And she said, 'Yes, I know it.'

And then I asked her, 'Then why, O why, would you want to be a prostitute?'

And she gave me this reply, 'Because I'm hungry.'

So I said to her, 'Don't carry on in prostitution. Instead, come here every day, and whatever food God provides for me, I will share with you.'

And so we continued in that way as long as I remained in that place.

And sometimes they came in with no friendly intent, as in the following:

An Impertinent Boy (160)

Father Paul, the abbot of father Theognosti's monastery, related a tale he had from an old hermit who had told it to him:

One day I was sitting in my cell with my handwork. At the time I was weaving baskets and singing the psalms as I worked. All of a sudden a small black boy jumped through the window clad in a shoulder cloak.

Standing in front of me he began to dance, and when I continued singing my psalms he asked me, 'Old man, don't I dance beautifully?'

When I answered him never a word he asked again, 'Doesn't my dancing thrill you, old man?'

But still I gave him no answer at all. Then he said, 'Do you really imagine, unreverend father, that what you are doing here is anything that matters? I can tell you that, in singing Psalm 65, Psalm 66, and Psalm 67, you made a lot of mistakes.'

So I got up and bowed low before God, and with that he disappeared.

If you were a female hermit you might be liable to sexual harassment, as in this case:

The Drastic Cure (60)

While we were in Alexandria, a fellow-Christian told us this tale:

There was a certain nun who lived the solitary life within her own house, concentrating on things spiritual, with continual fastings, prayers and vigils. She was also a generous giver of charity.

But the Devil, that unwavering foe of the human race, couldn't endure the sight of all the virgin's good deeds, and so he stirred up a dust storm against her. He planted in one of the young men a demon-inspired lust to have her.

The young man loitered outside her house. Whenever the nun wanted to come out of the house to go to chapel for prayer, this man would not leave her alone, harassing and pressing her, just as those obsessed by lust usually behave. Such was the harassment of this young man that the nun was compelled to stay inside her house, never going out.

Then one day the nun sent her little handmaid to tell the young man, 'Come! My mistress wants you.'

The young man took off with great rejoicing, thinking he had attained his goal.

The nun was seated before her loom, and she greeted him, 'Sit down.' And when they were seated she went on, 'Tell me the truth, dear brother, why are you harassing me in this way, not even allowing me to go out of my house?'

And his reply was, 'Truly Ma'am, I deeply, deeply desire you. The very sight of you just sets me ablaze.'

And then she said, 'But what beauty can you see in me that makes you desire me so?'

'It's your eyes; they have cast a spell on me.'

When the nun heard that it was her eyes that had ensnared the young man, she at once took her weaver's shuttle and dug out those eyes and threw both of them down before him.

When the young man saw that because of him the nun had cast away both her eyes, he repented and went off to a monastery where he became a steadfast monk.

But, even if left undisturbed, the hermit might be haunted by his past history:

The Haunted Monk (166)

This tale is from the father Sabbatios. He said that one day while he was staying in the monastery of the father Ferminos, a certain gangster came to see the father Zosimos the Cilician, and began to plead with him, 'Truly, I have been guilty of many killings, but now, for the love of God, make me a monk, so that for the rest of my life I can cease from all my crimes.'

The father first of all admonished him, and then made him a monk and provided him with the monastic habit. But a few days later, the father spoke to him again, 'Trust me, my boy, there is no way you can stay in this monastery. If the governor hears about it, he will arrest you, or if your enemies should turn up, they will put you to death. Listen to what I am telling you. I will take you to a community far away from here.'

And so he did. Ferminos took him to the community of the father Dorotheus near Gaza and Maiouma. There the man stayed for nine years. He learned all the psalms off by heart, and all the manners and customs of the monastic life.

But after that, he went back to the father Ferminos and told him, 'Father abbot, out of your love for me, I beg you, to give me back my secular clothes, and I will turn in my monastic habit.'

The old man was grieved to hear this, and asked him, 'Why is this, my son?'

To which the reply was, 'As you well know, father, I have lived for nine years in this community. I have fasted; I have kept the rule of chastity. In a quiet spirit and in the fear of God I have lived under this rule, and I have come to know that God, out of his abundant loving-kindness, has forgiven me all my so many crimes, and yet, still, every day, I see a little child who seems to say to me, 'Why, O why did you murder me?' I see this child in my dreams. I see him in the church. I see him in the refectory. Always saying the same words, he never leaves me for an hour. That is why I want to go back, father, so that I can die because of this little child; for it is true, I did murder him without any reason or cause.'

Then he took his secular clothes, put them on, and left the monastery to return to Nikopolis. The very next day he was arrested and beheaded.

It would seem that these desert monks were more Bible-based in their devotions than we often realize, if the following story is anything to go by:

Precious Bible (134)

There was a hermit in the Jordan region called Theodore. This man visited me in my cell one day and said, 'I'm begging a favour, Father John. See if you can find me a book that contains within it the whole of the New Testament.'

I had a look around and discovered that father Peter, the one who later became bishop of Chalcedon, had such a book. So I went to him, told him my quest, and he showed me this book, very beautifully bound.

'How much is it?' I asked.

And he answered, 'Three pounds.'

And then he asked me, 'Are you buying it for yourself or for someone else?'

And so I told him the whole story, 'Trust me, father, it is for a certain hermit who was asking me for it.'

And father Peter said, 'If it is a hermit who wants it, give it to him for nothing. In fact, here are three pounds. If he is satisfied with the book he can keep it; if he is not satisfied, use this three pounds to buy him whatever he wants.' So I took the book and delivered it to the hermit Theodore, who went off with it into the desert.

Two months later, he visited me a second time in my cell. 'You must realize, father John, that I have a very great scruple that is worrying me; it is this; the book cost me nothing.'

So I said, 'Don't fret. The father Peter is a very rich man, and a good one. He likes to do this sort of thing.'

But the hermit replied, 'Nevertheless I won't rest easy until I have paid the price.' So I asked him if he had the means to pay the price.

'No way! But give me a piece of sackcloth to wear.' For you see, he was completely naked.

So I gave him a piece of sackcloth and an old cloak and he went to work as a labourer at the cistern which John, the Patriarch of Jerusalem, was having dug at Sinai. He worked for about five pence a day, and later on he visited me at the monastery of the Aiolians. He was eating only ten small turnips a day. He worked without ceasing until the pennies he saved had made up the three pounds.

That day he said, 'Take these bits and pieces and give them to the man. If he won't accept them, then give him back the book.'

So I went to father Peter and told him all this. He was unhappy about taking either the pennies or the book back again, but I compelled him to accept the pennies so as not to slight the hard labour of the hermit. He then took the money and I delivered the book to Theodore who then returned, full of joy, into the desert.

On the other hand the phenomenon of the 'liberated monk' had already begun to appear:

A Liberated Monk (194)

There was one old father living in a cell of the monastery who had to go up to Alexandria to sell his handiwork. While there, he saw a young monk going into a bar. The old man was so deeply shocked by the sight that he waited outside to catch him when he came out.

Then the old monk took the young one's hand and led him aside to say, 'Dear brother, don't you realize that you are wearing the holy habit? Don't you realize that you are still only a youth? Don't you realize how many are the traps that the devil lays before us? Don't you realize that it is through the eyes, through the ears, and through the glamour of the world that monks are irretrievably damaged as they walk the city streets? But you! You go into a bar of your own free will, and hear there what you should not want to hear, and see what you should not want to see, and mix so casually with the women. Such is not the way. Fly back, I beg you, to the desert and there find the salvation you long for.'

The young monk answered him, 'On your way, reverend father. For what does God ask of us? Nothing more than a pure heart.'

Then the old father reached out his arms to the heavens and said, 'Glory to thee, O God, glory to thee. For fifty years I have been living in my cell and have not yet managed to attain to purity of heart, while this young man, the regular frequenter of bars, has already attained purity of heart.'

And turning to the brother he said, 'May God bring you to salvation, and may I not be disappointed of my hope.'

PILLAR SAINTS

In a religious climate that fostered all kinds of extremes, those men and women who spent years and years of their lives living on the tops of pillars, drew great crowds of admiring people who came to witness the advice they handed out to troubled souls, and to watch for the miracles they might perform. The counselling was done thus:

Stylite Stories (129)

The father Athanasius told us a tale he had from the bishop of Petra, Athenogenes.

We had a stylite in our region to whom many people used to go for consultations. They did this standing at the base of his column, for he had no ladder.

One day a brother told him, 'I have a problem I would like to discuss with you.'

And in the gentlest of voices, the holy man replied, 'Go over to the other side of the platform, the part beneath my sleeping place.'

And so he went over to the other corner of the platform and that was how the two of them conversed with one another, the saint from above, the brother from below, and none of those standing around heard what they said.

Another story about the same stylite:

There were two herdsmen who were very deeply attached to one another, and they visited the stylite many times over the years, but they never came separately, always together. But it happened that one day one of them did show up without having informed his companion. He stood knocking at the gate for many hours, but the father refused to admit him. Overcome by weariness, the man turned back.

On his return journey he was met by his companion who was on his way to visit the stylite himself. Back they went again so that both together could see the stylite. When they knocked at the gate, the father beckoned the last comer to enter alone.

When he went in, he began to plead with the father to admit his companion, but the old father said, 'I cannot receive him.'

And when the man continued to plead with him, he added, 'My son, I cannot receive a person whom God has turned back.'

These men often had remarkable insights into the hearts of those gathered below them, as in this case:

The Offending Eye (118)

The father Sergius from Raithou told us this tale about one of their brothers there, Menas by name, a deacon.

One day this brother went out into the city on some business or other, and whatever happened to him that day we never found out. But when he came back, he took off his monastic habit and went back to being a civilian again. Quite a long time later he had to go up to Antioch, and as he was passing through Seleucia he saw in the distance the community of that saint of God, Simon the Stylite. So he said to himself, 'I will go and see the great Simon, for I have never yet in my life set eyes on him.'

So he went. But as he got closer to the pillar, the father Simon saw him coming and recognized both that he was a monk and that he had received ordination as a deacon. So he called to his serving man, 'Fetch me the scissors.'

And when they had brought them he said, 'Praise the Lord and give that man a tonsure,'—pointing out with his finger our man amidst the crowd milling around the pillar. The man was astounded at such a development and, trembling and shaking, he accepted his shearing without a word, for he realized that God had uncovered his whole story to the saint.

Then the father Simon said to him, 'Now, sing the deacon's litany.'

And when he had done so, the saint told him, 'Go back to where you came from. Go back to Raithou.'

But when the man explained how full of shame he was, so much so, that he could no longer look his brothers in the eye, the saint spoke again, 'Trust me, my boy, there is no need for shame any longer. The fathers there will receive you with smiles on their faces and hearts full of joy and gladness at your return.'

And then he added, 'God is going to give you a sign that he has forgiven you all that sin of yours.'

When the man reached Raithou, the fathers there did indeed welcome him with outstretched arms, and restored him to his place in the choir.

Then one Sunday, as he was carrying in procession the holy and life-giving blood of our great God and Saviour, Jesus Christ, all at once one of his eyes fell out, and then everyone knew from this sign (Matt. 5: 29) that God had forgiven him his sin, just as the righteous Simon said he would.

But even so, the stylite monks did not manage to avoid all the religious controversies of the day:

Pillar News (36)

One of the priests attached to the Patriarch Ephraim of Antioch told us this story.

Ephraim was a very fiery man and a hot defender of orthodoxy. He heard one day about a certain pillar monk in the Hierapolis region who had gone over to the heresy of the Severians and was now one of that excommunicated band.

The godly Ephraim set off in haste to see him because he hoped to win him back. As soon as he got to the pillar he began to exhort the stylite and urged him to lose no time in returning to the Holy Catholic and Apostolic Church.

But the stylite called down, 'I am no longer in communion with that synod of yours.'

To which Ephraim replied, 'Then what kind of reconciliation procedure do you suggest I might offer to you? After all, the holy church, thanks to Jesus Christ our Lord and God, has now been liberated from every spot of heretical teaching.'

To which the stylite made this suggestion: 'Yes, my Lord Patriarch, kindle a fire and then let you and I go in it together, and whichever comes out the other side unharmed, he will be the orthodox one and we must follow that man.'

Ephraim murmured, 'It would be rather more appropriate that you, my son, should pay attention to my words, rather than making further conditions, conditions, moreover, that go well beyond the strength of a wretch like me. However, taking my courage from the mercies of God and remembering that your life depends on it, I will do what you ask.'

And turning to the bystanders, he said, 'Blessed be God. Bring us some wood.'

When the wood had been gathered, the patriarch lit the fire at the foot of the pillar. Then he said, 'Time for you to come down! And we will go in together as you decided.'

But the stylite, voiceless now at the patriarch's steadfast faith in God, decided that he no longer wished to come down.

So the patriarch called to him, 'Was it not you who proposed this test just a few minutes ago? Why have you changed your mind?'

Then the archbishop took off his Episcopal stole and standing beside the fire he prayed, 'Lord Jesus, our Christ and our God, it was for our sake that you chose in the holy mother of God, the ever-virgin Mary to become a fully human person; show us now the truth here.'

The prayer completed, he shoved his stole into the middle of the fire. Then, after the fire had burned about three hours and the wood was all used up, he took his stole out of the fire, unharmed and whole with not even a scorch mark on it. When the stylite saw what had happened he was fully persuaded, and he renounced Severus and all his heretical ways and adjourned to the holy church where he received the sacrament at the hands of the saintly Ephraim and there he gave God all the glory.

Nevertheless, the common people don't seem to have had an undue or excessive reverence for these holy men. They were not afraid to rebuke them, if necessary.

The Trespassers (218)

Father Sergius, the prior of Abbot Constantine's monastery, told me:

Once some of us were out walking with a certain very holy father, and we wandered off the path without realizing it, and with no thought as to where we were going. We found ourselves stumbling about in a wheat field and trampling down some of the wheat.

The farmer, who was at work in the field, saw what we were doing and began to shout at us in a very insolent way, 'You people! Are you monks? Do you have no fear of God in you? If you had the fear of God before your eyes, you would not be doing what you are doing now.'

Straightway our saintly companion said to us, 'For the Lord's sake, none of you answer him.'

And then he began, 'You are quite right, my son; if we had the fear of God we would not be here.'

But the farmer, still in a temper, continued to insult them. Our father answered him a second time, 'You are only speaking the truth, my son; if only we were true monks we would not have done such a thing.'

The farmer was cut to the quick by these words, and he came and knelt down at our father's feet, 'I am a sinner; please forgive me, and, for the Lord's sake, take me with you.'

The saintly Sergius concluded, 'It is true. That farmer fell in with us and later on was given the holy habit.'

PERILS AND DANGERS OF TRAVEL

Travel in the Byzantine world was never easy and seldom safe. Perils at sea from pirates, perils on land from brigands and perils on both land and sea from storms, floods and desert sands. And this is not to mention those ill-intentioned spirits hovering over your path, ready to strike when you were most vulnerable, as this sea captain's case illustrates:

The Sea-Captain's Test (76)

It was Palladius who told us this story, which he had from a ship's captain he had met. This man told him about a trip he had made with a shipload of passengers, both men and women.

There was a fair wind behind them and everything was perfect for sailing on the open sea. Some were sailing for Constantinople, some for Alexandria, and others to any port you could mention. However, we were becalmed.

For fifteen days we stuck in the same spot, unable to move from the place, We all became extremely anxious and full of worries about what might be the possible cause. After all, I, as captain, was responsible for the whole ship and all who sailed in it. So I began to pray to God for help.

One day, a bodiless voice rang in my ear, 'Throw Mary overboard and you will be all right.'

So I made a little experiment; I shouted at the top of my lungs, 'Mary!' though I didn't know who Mary was.

Then one of the women stood up in the berth where she was lying and answered me, 'Sir? What do you want?'

And I said, 'Be so good as to come up here.'

She got up and came to me, and I took her aside and said to her, 'Mary, my sister, you can now see what great sins are mine, for it is because of me that all on board this ship will have to perish.'

She gave a groan from the depths of her heart and said, 'Captain, sir, I am the one who is the sinner.'

'My dear,' I said, 'what are these sins of yours?'

'Woe is me, there is no sin that I have not committed, and it is because of me that you will all perish. To tell the truth, Captain, sir, I am an accursed woman. I had a husband and we had two children, the one was nine years old, the other five. Then my husband died and I was left a widow. There happened to be a soldier living next door to us, and I longed for him to marry me. I sent some friends to negotiate, but the soldier said, "I will never marry a woman with another man's children."

'When I heard he wouldn't marry me because of the children, yet being still madly in love with him, I took the children, cut their throats and sent him word. "See, I have no encumbrances now."

'When the soldier heard what I had done to the children, he swore, "By the living God whose dwelling is in heaven, I will never marry her."

'Then, as the whole business became known, I ran away for fear of my life.'

Even yet, said the captain, even after I had heard her story, I was very reluctant to throw her into the sea, so I devised this test. I said, 'Look, I am now going to get into the small boat and row off from the ship. Then, if the ship begins to move, we will know that it is my sins that are holding us back.'

So I ordered out the small boat and got down into it, but nothing happened; neither the ship nor the small boat moved an inch.

So I climbed back into the ship and told the woman, 'Now it is your turn to get down into the small boat.'

She did so, and immediately that small boat made five small circles and went straight down to the bottom. Our ship then sailed on its way, and in three and a half days we covered more distance than in the whole of the previous fifteen days.

Nor were your crew always to be depended on!

What Price Life? (203)

One of the fathers told us this story about a jeweller who also did some gem engraving. Taking with him many of his precious stones and pearls, he had boarded a ship with his servants with the intention of going abroad and engaging in his trade there.

In the providence of God it happened that this man fell in love with the ship's cabin boy, who acted as a servant. The boy used to rest at his side and shared his table with him. One day the boy heard the sailors whispering amongst themselves and plotting to throw the engraver into the sea for the sake of the jewels he had with him. As a result the boy fell into the deepest gloom when he went to wait on his master as he usually did.

So the master said, 'Why so downcast today, my boy?' But the boy held his grief in check and said nothing.

So again the jeweller asked him, 'Tell me the truth, what's the matter?' Then the boy burst into tears and told him all, 'This and this is the plot the sailors have hatched against you.'

'Are you sure?' the jeweller asked.

And he answered, 'Yes indeed, this is what they have plotted between them to do to you.'

Then the jeweller summoned his servants and told them, 'Whatever I command you to do, do it at once, without even thinking.'

Then he spread out a sheet on the deck and told them, 'Bring me here my jewel cases.' And they brought them.

Then he opened them and spread out all the stones on the sheet where all could see them, and this is what he said: 'Is this what my life is worth? Is it for the sake of these stones that I risk my life, and battle over stormy seas, only, very shortly, to lay down this life, and take with me out of this world not a single thing?'

Then he said to his servants, 'Empty the sheet into the sea.'

No sooner had he spoken than they hurled the whole lot into the sea. That is how the sailors were foiled and their plot smashed.

Occasionally, though, you might find sheep in wolves' clothing!

The Sinners' Friends (165)

One of Christ's followers told us this tale about a gangster called Cyriac, who roamed about in the region of Emmaus, that is, Nikopolis. This gangster was so cruel, so inhuman, that they used to call him the Wolf. He had a number of other criminals along with him, not just Christians, but Jews and Samaritans as well.

One day at the beginning of Holy Week, a party came from one of the farms of Nikopolis, on their way to the holy city of Jerusalem to have their little ones baptized. When the baptisms had been completed and they were on their way home to keep the holy feast of the Resurrection there, the gangsters fell upon them; though that day they did not have the Wolf with them.

The men of the party at once took to their heels, but the women were grabbed, their babies tossed aside, and they were raped by the Jews and Samaritans. Meanwhile, the men in their flight were met by the gangster chief, who asked the reason for their haste, and they told him what had happened. He then took them and led them back to his mates. When he saw the little ones lying about on the ground, he inquired as to who was responsible. Then and there he beheaded the perpetrators of the crime. He then ordered the men to pick up the children (since the women, now defiled, could no longer touch them), and he led them all home in safety.

Some time after this incident, the gangster chief was arrested and locked up in prison for ten years, but he was never put to death. Later on, after he had been released, he always used to say, 'It is because of those children that I escaped a bitter death. I used to see them in my dreams saying to me, "Don't be afraid, we are pleading on your behalf."'

Both the father John of the monastery of the Eunuchs and I met this man and heard the whole story from him, whereupon we gave God the glory.

Sometimes, in desert crossings, things became very desperate, and there was danger of dying from thirst:

Baptism by Sand (176)

When we were in Alexandria, the father Andrew, whom we met there, told us this tale:

When I was still a young man and completely carefree, a time of civil unrest and rioting arose in Alexandria, so I and nine others set off for Palestine. One of our band was a working man, and one was a Hebrew. While we were still in the desert, the Hebrew lad became very sick; in fact, he appeared to be dying, and we fell into the depths of despair, with no idea of what we could do for him. But we refused to forsake him, so each one in turn, while his strength lasted, carried the lad along, hoping to reach some town or market so that he would not die alone in the desert.

But when the lad, through lack of food, raging fever, complete exhaustion and the heat-induced thirst, became completely helpless and was in a state of total collapse, there seemed to be nothing left for him but to depart his life; for, in truth, he could no longer endure even to be carried. We then decided with tears in our eyes that we would have to leave him in the desert and press on ourselves, bearing in mind that death from thirst was likely to overtake us, too.

As we laid him down in the sand, and he saw from our tears that we were preparing to leave him, he began to invoke God and to plead with us, 'By the God who will surely judge the living and the dead, do not leave me to die as a Hebrew; let me, I beg, die as a Christian. Show me this mercy and baptize me so that I may depart this life as a Christian and thus go to be with God.'

But we answered him, 'Truly, dear brother, we cannot do such a thing. We are laymen, and that is a job for bishops and priests, and besides all that, there is no water here.'

But he persisted with the same imprecations and copious tears to plead with us, 'Christian brothers, do not deprive me of such a gift as this.'

While we were still mired in the depths of our quandary, the working man, moved by God, spoke up, 'Stand him up on his feet and strip off his clothes.' And so with the greatest difficulty we got him upright and stripped off his clothes.

Then the working man filled his hands with sand, and three times poured it over the sick man's head with the words, 'Theodore is baptized in the name of the Father and of the Son and of the Holy Spirit.'

And we bystanders said the Amen at each name of the holy, consubstantial, and ever to be adored Trinity. Then, and this is the Lord's truth my brothers, Christ the son of the living God did there heal him, and so restored his strength that not a trace of his former weakness now remained. Rather, in the full vigour of health, with rosy cheeks and boundless enthusiasm, he walked on ahead of us through whatever remained of our desert journey.

When we arrived at Ascalon, we told the full story of all that had befallen our brother on the way to the right reverend, the blessed Dionysius, the bishop of the place.

When the blessed Dionysius heard the tale, he became very thoughtful at such an unprecedented miracle. Thus he called together the whole body of the clergy and placed before them this question, whether the pouring of sand could be reckoned as a true baptism or not.

Some said, 'Yes, it must be reckoned as valid because of the stupendous nature of the miracle which followed from it.'

But others said, 'No, because Gregory (Nazianzus) the theologian enumerated for us all the kinds of baptism: first there is the baptism of Moses, but that was water baptism, because it says previously that he was baptized in the cloud and in the sea. Then there is the baptism of John, but that was more than a Jewish rite, for he didn't simply baptize with water, he baptized unto repentance. Then Jesus baptized, but that was with the Holy Spirit, and that is the highest form of baptism. Then we also know a fourth kind of baptism, that which comes with the shedding of blood in martyrdom; and there is even a fifth kind of baptism, that which comes through tears shed. Now, which of these kinds of baptism describes the case of this young man so that we may confirm it? Moreover, we need to bear in mind the Lord's words to Nicodemus, "Unless one is born of water and the Spirit, he cannot enter the kingdom of heaven."'

Immediately, new voices raised other objections, saying, 'There is no record that any of the apostles were baptized; so, are they not going to enter the kingdom of heaven?'

Then conflicting arguments were brought out to oppose these men, 'Indeed and in truth they, the apostles, were baptized as Clement Stromateus tells us in volume five of his book on typology. When he is there explaining that text of the apostle's, "I give thanks that I baptized none of you", he says it means that Christ baptized none of the apostles but Peter, and that then Peter baptized Andrew, Andrew baptized James and John, and then they baptized all the rest.'

These and countless other arguments were all discussed at length until his reverence, Bishop Dionysius, made his decision. The young man was sent down to the holy river Jordan, there to be baptized.

And as for that working man, the bishop at once ordained him deacon.

But not all travellers' tales had such complicated endings:

Athirst at Sea (174)

The father Gregory the hermit told us this tale:

When I was coming back from Byzantium, I went on board ship with a businessman and his wife, who were intending to pray in the holy city of Jerusalem. The captain of the vessel was a religious man and a frequent faster.

Once at sea, the servants of the businessman distributed our water in a free and easy way so that by the time we reached mid-voyage, the water was all gone and we were in real trouble. It was a pitiful sight to see the women, the children, and even small babies prostrate with thirst, and lying about as if they were dead. This disaster gripped us for three days and we had lost all hope of life.

The pain was more than the businessman could bear, and he drew his sword, intending to kill the captain first and then the crew, for he said, 'It is the fault of these men that we are perishing; they are the ones who failed to take on board sufficient water for our needs.'

But I shouted to the man, 'Don't do it! Pray instead to our Lord Jesus Christ, our one true God who works innumerable miracles far beyond our expectations. Look! You can see for yourself that our captain here has been fasting for three days now, and has been spending all his time in prayer.'

After this the businessman calmed down. The next day about noon, the captain stood up on his feet and cried with a mighty shout, 'Glory to you, Christ our God,' so that we were all speechless at his cry.

Then he said to the crew, 'Take down the awnings at once.' And no sooner had they folded back the awnings than a cloud rolled over the ship and rained down upon us such an abundance of water as to supply all our needs.

There also followed this strange, awesome phenomenon: as the ship got under way again, the cloud remained over us and shed its rain only on our ship, and nowhere else.

CHILDREN

Children seldom appear in these tales of the fathers, but the youngest child to appear made an important statement in his day, to the astonishment of all:

A Wise Child (114)

The same old father told us this next tale about the father Daniel, the Egyptian:

One day Daniel went up to Terenouth to sell his basket-work. There a young man came up to him, 'Reverend Father, for God's sake come to my house and say your prayers over my wife. She is barren.'

The father, persuaded against his will by the young man, went back to his house with him and performed the prayers over the wife. Later, by God's will, she conceived.

However, there were some ill-natured scoundrels who began to gossip about our father, whispering, 'The truth is, the young man is still childless; that baby is Father Daniel's.'

This rumour reached the father's ears, and he sent a message to the woman's husband, 'When your wife gives birth, let me know at once.'

And when the woman gave birth, her husband sent a message back to Daniel straight away, 'Through God and through your prayers, father, she has borne a child.'

Then father Daniel went out and advised the young husband, 'Make a great feast and invite all your kinfolk and all your friends.'

While they were all sitting round the table, our father took the baby in his arms and, in the hearing of all there, he asked the baby, 'Who is your father?'

And the baby with the finger of his little hand pointed to the young man and said, 'HIM.' The baby was only twenty-two days old at the time.

They all gave the glory to God who preserves in the truth those that seek him with their whole hearts

But there were also some children who showed a precocious knowledge of liturgy and theology, as in this case:

Playing Mass (196)

George was an African man from the region of Apameia, the second province of Syria. He was a great lover of Christ, and also of the monks and of the poor. He told us this tale:

At my place there is a village called Gonagas; it is about forty miles from the city, and then a mile or so further still beyond Gonagas, there lie some hills where the local boys used to herd their sheep. And as always, boys will be boys; so it happened that these boys never tired of playing one game or another.

One day, as they played, they said to one another, 'Come on! Let's make a mass and offer an offering.'

This seemed like a great idea to all of them, and straightway they chose one of their number to take the part of the priest, and another two to be the deacons. They found a rock which had a flat top, and the game began. On the rock which served as their altar they set out the bread and, in a little earthenware cup, their wine. Then they took their places, the priest in the centre and the deacons on either side. One boy said the offertory prayers, and the others waved bundles of leaves as fans. It appears that the so-called priest knew the whole prayer of consecration, since it was the normal custom in their church for the children to stand right at the front at the entrance to the sanctuary, and they were the first, after the clergy, to receive the holy mysteries. Now apparently the priest in that church used to say the mass in a loud clear voice, with the result that these boys, from constantly hearing it, had learned the whole of the prayer of consecration by heart.

After they had completed everything according to the rites of the church, but before they broke the bread, fire fell from heaven and consumed the whole offering and blasted the whole rock, so that not the slightest fragment of the rock or of what had been offered on it remained. It was over in an instant, and at the sight the boys fell terrified to the ground and lay there half dead. Struck dumb with terror, they were completely unable to get back on their feet.

When they didn't return to the village at their usual hour of home-coming, their parents set out to see why they had not come back. After some searching they found them flat out on the ground. The boys couldn't recognize any of those who had come for them, nor were they able to speak to any of those who were speaking to them.

When the parents saw their children half dead like this, each one picked up his own child and carried him back to the village. The sight of their children so changed greatly changed the parents as well, more especially as they couldn't discover what had brought about such a state. All that day they kept questioning them over and over, but answer there was none. They could get no information about what had happened. It was only after a whole day and a whole night had gone by that the children returned to their senses, bit by bit, and told them everything—what had happened and why it had happened. Then they took their parents and the other villagers as well, and led them to the place and pointed out to them where this miracle had occurred, for you could still see the marks where the fire had fallen.

Some of the parents, after hearing the tale, were convinced by these proofs that they were telling the truth, and they went straightway to their bishop and told him the whole story from start to finish. The bishop was astonished at such a miracle and set off at once with all his clergy. As soon as he had seen the boys and questioned them about what had happened, and seen the marks of the fire from heaven, the first thing he did was to pack the boys off to a monastery, and then he himself had a new monastery erected on the very spot where the fire had struck.

This same George told us he had himself seen one of those boys in that very monastery where the miracle had taken place.

Such is the tale that George, the Christ-lover, told us about this heavenly miracle.

The boyhood of the great Athanasius was remarkable too:

The Boyhood of Athanasius (197)

Rufinus, the great church historian, has recorded a similar incident from bygone days involving children and their games. He has this tale to tell about the childhood days of St Athanasius the great, that battler for and proclaimer of the truth, the foremost citizen of the great city of Alexandria, the one who shepherded his whole flock according to the judgements of God. Rufinus makes it clear in his description of the saint's childhood that his advance to the top was ordained by God from the first, originating as it did in the providence of God. Therefore I have decided to retell the early life of this great man: what sort of boy he was, what sort of upbringing he had. This tradition which has been handed on to me, I now present to you.

In those days the blessed Alexander was the pope of Alexandria; he came after Achilles, just as the saintly Peter the archbishop and martyr, the one who condemned the blasphemous, had said that he would do. One day Alexander was gazing out to sea from a small rise in the land, when he noticed some boys, playing down on the beach, as boys always do. They seemed to be imitating a bishop and all the customary rites that take place in the church.

As he observed them for some time, he saw that even those mysteries that are hidden from the public gaze were being performed by them. He was very upset. First of all he summoned his clergy and told them what the boys were doing, and he ordered them to go and round them all up and bring them before him.

When they came, he questioned them closely, 'What game is this? What do you think you are doing?'

The children were terrified and, like all children, at first they denied everything; but afterward they confessed the whole business in detail. The boys said that under Athanasius, whom they had chosen to be their bishop, they had baptised some catechumens. Then Alexander questioned them further, 'Whom have you baptised? What questions did you put to the candidates? And what answers did they give?'

He thus discovered that they had indeed fulfilled all the rites and customs of the liturgy. He called a chapter of his clergy and decreed that those who had in this way been brought to the sacred font did not need to be baptised a second time. Then he took Athanasius and the others whom they had named deacons and priests and entrusted them to their parents to bring up in the nurture and fear of the Lord. He was especially concerned with Athanasius, whom a little later he dedicated to God, and the boy, now enriched with a divine charism from the archbishop, stood out the more as a person of great depth and strength.

After a little time had passed, when Athanasius had mastered the art of writing and completed his basic education, his parents handed him back to the priest, as a faithful charge laid upon them by God, and the boy, like the infant Samuel, was now reared in the temple. When Alexander in his old age needed to visit various bishops, Athanasius would go with him to carry his priestly vestment, which in the Hebrew language is called the *ephod*.

So many and so great were the battles undertaken by this Athanasius against the heretics in the church that it seems that this text must have been written especially to be applied to him: 'I will show him what things he must endure for the sake of my name' (Acts 9:16).

For the whole earth joined as one in the persecution of this man. Kings of the earth, nations and armies moved together against him, but he never deviated from the word of God. 'Though an army encamp against me, yet my heart shall not be afraid, And though war should rise up against me, yet will I put my trust in him' (Ps. 27:3).

So many and so critical were the accomplishments of this man that on the grounds of their importance I cannot be excused if I exclude anything, but such is the quantity of the material available, I am forced to leave some things unrecorded. In fact my mind is in a complete whirl, trying to distinguish between what must be kept and what has to be omitted. That is why we have recorded just a few things from the material that has reached us. As for all the rest, we will have to leave that to word of mouth. But word of mouth will always fall short of the whole story, nor will it ever be able to find ways of adding anything to the truth.

SAINTS AND SINNERS

It is highly probable that the last hours of the arch-heretic Arius formed a staple of conversation and gossip in many monastic common rooms for several generations; so much so that copy-cat deaths soon began to appear, one of which came to the ears of John Moschus:

A Privy Death (43)

There was once an archbishop in Thessalonica by the name of Thalelaios. This man showed no respect for God, nor fear of the retribution that was waiting for him. That little man trampled under foot the Christian teachings and reckoned as nothing the dignity of the priesthood. In truth he was more like a ravening wolf than a shepherd. He refused (God preserve us!) to worship the holy and undivided Trinity and bowed to idols.

Those who held authority in the church in those days took a lawful vote on the matter and deposed him from his office. However, within a very short time, that same man, crammed full as he was with every corruption, was plotting to get back into his priestly office. And because, as the Wisdom of Solomon[1] tells us, 'all things give way to money', he was soon invited back, as of right, to his former see. This all took place in Constantinople, that home of the big men who, in the words of Isaiah the prophet, pronounce the guilty innocent for a bribe, and strip the righteous of his righteousness. (Is. 5: 23)

But God had not yet forgotten his church, for he again condemned as highly displeasing to him that vote in the man's favour which was passed contrary to the apostolic canons. It happened like this.

On the day he was decking himself out in his episcopal finery, just as he was on the verge of leaving his house, and

---

[1] This is, in fact, a quotation from Ecclesiastes 10:19.

preparing to sally forth to the rulers of the church to receive as his due his re-election to the holy priesthood, cramps in his belly drove him into the latrine. There he remained for about two hours without reappearing. Then some of his attendants who were waiting outside went to remind him that it was time to go, and they found him with his head stuck into the waste channel and his feet pointing up in the air.

The death he suffered was a perfect replica of that of the enemy of God, the blasphemous Arius, for that one too, in his megalomania put his confidence in the rulers of this world and planned to trample the church underfoot. Similarly, while Arius was in the privy, the Angel of Mighty Counsel, marvellous defender of the church of God, shattered his guts to bits, pregnant as they were with every kind of blasphemy.

It was the same with this man, who hoped by his nefarious tricks and with the help of those in authority to carry out measures even more oppressive than hitherto. Then that angel who is the patron of Thessalonica's church, along with the mighty martyr Demetrius, appeared at the very spot where, coupled with that foul demon, his aider and abettor, he was scheming new treachery against the church of God.

In that very place the angel transfixed the impiety of this useless servant. Those feet of his which had never learned to walk the straight path, were left waving in the air, bearing the clear marks of the divine judgement that was about to fall upon him, for it is indeed 'a fearful thing to fall into the hands of the living God' (Heb. 10: 31).

On the other hand, here is a saintly bishop who became a worker priest long before that vocation was even known or recognized:

The Worker Bishop (37)

One of the fathers told us a tale about a certain bishop who went to Antioch and there he gave up his bishopric and took to earning his living working in the building trade.

At the same time there was a man named Ephraim, a very compassionate and sympathetic man who lived in the eastern suburbs. It was due to this man's efforts that many of the public buildings in the city were being rebuilt after they had been devastated by a recent earthquake.

One night in a dream this Ephraim saw a bishop sound asleep with a pillar of fire rising above his head reaching right up to heaven. He had this dream not just once, but over and over again, and he could no way interpret it. However, it seemed to betoken something awesome and unsettling, and so he kept searching his mind for what it could possibly mean. But how could Ephraim have identified the bishop in this workman? How could he ever have recognized a bishop in this man who was just one of the crowd of workers? He was clad in filthy clothes, with unwashed hair, and utterly worn out by all he had to bear, by his meagre diet and his unremitting toil—not to mention the blows and beatings that came his way from all and sundry.

One day Ephraim sent for this workman who had once been a bishop, because he wanted to find out who he was. He began by asking, just between the two of them, where he came from and what his name was.

The man replied, 'I am just one of the poor folk of this city. Because I have no way of maintaining myself, I work, and God feeds me with my wages.'

Then Ephraim, inwardly moved by the Spirit, told him, 'Believe me, I will not let you go until you tell me the whole truth about yourself.'

Then the workman, unable to remain hidden any longer, said, 'Give me your word that you will not repeat my story and my present state of life to anyone. If you promise, I will give you the whole story, except for my name and the city I came from.'

Then the godly Ephraim swore an oath that he would never tell this story to anyone as long as God gave him life in this world.

'I am a bishop,' he said, 'who left off being a bishop for the sake of God, and came to this place, where I was completely unknown, to embrace the sufferings and the sweat of working men. By the sweat of my hands I provide for myself my scanty food to which, if you will, you could add a little extra. For shortly God is going to raise you up to the apostolic throne of this church of Antioch so that you might be a shepherd for these people whom Christ, our true God, has purchased with his own blood. So, as I have said, struggle hard for the poor and for the faith, for with such sacrifices God is well pleased.'

Within a few days it fell out just as the man had said. And at the end of the workman's story, Ephraim gave God the glory and said, 'How many hidden servants God has here; how many that are known to him alone.'

And here is the case of holiness achieved through loyal friendship:

Two Inseparable Brothers (97)

Father John, the anchorite, the one with red hair, told us of a tale he had heard from Father Stephan, the Moabite:

When I was living in the monastery of St Theodosius, that great master of monks, there were two brothers there who swore an oath of loyalty each to the other that neither in life nor in death would they be divided from one another. The unity of this pair strengthened and edified all the other brothers.

Then it happened one day that one brother was attacked by a great hunger for sex, and when he could endure the battle no longer, he said to his brother, 'My brother, let me go. I am overwhelmed with a hunger for sex, and so now I am determined to leave here and go back to the city.'

His brother began to plead with him, 'Please, my brother, don't destroy now all the good work you have done so far.'

But he replied, 'Either you come with me until I find some way of meeting my sexual need, or release me from my vow and let me go alone.'

His brother could not bring himself to release him, and so he went with him to the city. The tempted man went into a brothel, while the other brother stood in the street outside, taking handfuls of dirt from the ground and pouring them over his head, so humiliated did he feel himself to be.

When the other brother came out of the brothel, having done what he came to do, his brother said, 'How much better off are you now from this business? Have you not rather suffered a grievous loss? Come on, let's go back home.'

'No,' he replied, 'I can't go back to the desert. You go and I will stay on in town.'

In spite of all that he could say, his brother could not persuade him to return to the desert, so he himself stayed in town with him. To feed themselves, they both got jobs as labourers

Then along came Father Abram, who was a really good and gentle shepherd. Earlier on he had established the monastery of the Abramites in Constantinople, and later on he was to be made bishop of Ephesus, but at this time he was building his own monastery in this place. It was to be called the monastery of the Byzantines.

The two brothers began to work as labourers on this site and drew their wages. The one who had become sex-obsessed, however, would take the pay packet of both and run off into town each day to blow the lot on 'good times'. The other brother used to fast each day, and did his work faithfully, with no manner of fuss. He didn't talk a lot to anyone.

When his mates on the job noticed his behaviour, how he ate seldom, spoke seldom and always seemed to be meditating on something, they went and told Father Abram about him and his manner of life.

The father then summoned the workman to his office, and questioned him, 'Where are you from, my brother? What is your trade?'

The man then confessed to the whole business: 'It's for the sake of my brother that I live this life of hard toil. My hope is that God who sees my afflictions will save my brother's life.'

When the godly Abram heard it all, he replied, 'Yes indeed, and surely now the Lord will return to you the life of your brother.'

And look: just as he was leaving the cell of father Abram, there was his brother calling out to him, 'Dear brother, take me back to the desert before I lose my life altogether.'

At once they both returned to their hermitage beside the sacred Jordan, and the wayward brother was once again enclosed. Within a relatively short time, by God's help, he made great advances in the spiritual realm, and then departed to be with the Lord. The other brother, still loyal to his oath, lived on in the same hermitage until he too had completed his course

But not everyone was a monk. There were countless other ways that people found to earn their way through life:

Three Blind Men (77)

One day I and master Sophronius dropped in at midday at the house of Professor Stephen for a short seminar together. He was then staying at that church of the holy Mother of God which the blessed Pope Eulogius had built, the one often referred to as 'God's Gift'.

When we knocked on the philosopher's door, the maid peeked out and said, 'He is sleeping. Come back a little later.'

So then I said to master Sophronius, 'Let's go down to the Four Gates and wait there.' This district, the Four Gates, is reckoned by the people of Alexandria to be a very special spot. They say that Alexander the Great, their city's founder, brought the bones of Jeremiah the prophet from Egypt and laid them up at this place.

When we arrived at the place, since it was high noon, we found it quite deserted except for three blind men. We went over to the corner where the blind men were, and sat down quietly without any fuss nearby. We had our books to read.

The blind men were in conversation, and one of them said to the others, 'Tell the truth now. How did you become blind?'

To which one of them answered, 'When I was a young man I was a sailor, and while we were sailing from Africa in the middle of the sea, I was stricken with ophthalmia. At sea there was no way that I could receive any treatment for the white patches which began covering my eyes, and so I became blind.'

Then he asked the next man, 'How about you? How did you become blind?'

And he replied, 'I was a glass-blower by trade, and the blast of the fire struck on both my eyes, and thus I became blind.'

Then those two asked the third man, 'How about you? How did you become blind?'

And he replied, 'Now indeed I will tell you the whole truth. When I was a young man I hated all manner of work, and so I became nothing but a playboy. When all my food ran out, I turned to stealing. One day when I was standing in the market, with a number of petty thefts already to my credit, I saw a corpse being carried past, magnificently dressed. I fell in at the rear of the procession to see where they would bury it. They went to the back of the church of St John and placed him in a tomb there and departed.[2]

'When I saw the coast was clear, I went into the tomb and stripped the body of all the clothes he wore, leaving him only in his underwear. Just as I was about to leave the tomb with all my loot, my evil nature nudged me and said, 'Why not take the underwear as well? It's top class stuff.'

So, fool that I was, I went back in. But as I was stripping him of his underwear to leave him stark naked, the corpse sat up in front of me and, reaching out, grabbed me with both hands, and then with his fingers he dug out my sight and threw my two eyes to the ground.

Then I, unluckiest of men, forsook all my loot, and, wracked with pain and still in danger, I ran from the tomb. There, now, I have told you how I became blind.'

When we had heard all these stories, master Sophronius nodded silently to me, and as we were going quietly away, he said, 'Let's not have any further conferences today, for we have already learned a great deal.'

And what we learned that day we have written down so that you too may hear and learn the same lesson from men who had experienced its truth.

---

[2] The bodies of the wealthy were generally placed in a stone sarcophagus complete with stone lid, all elaborately carved.

Even apparently hopeless sinners came to repentance, sometimes in unexpected ways, as in this case:

The Grave Robber's Tale and the Value of Confession (78)

Father John, who was abbot of the Gigantes monastery in Antioch, told us a similar tale to this when we visited him:

A short while ago, a young man came to me and said, 'In the name of God receive me here, for I want now to live a life of penitence.' As he spoke, the tears streamed down.

I asked him, 'Tell me, my son, what is it that has worked such great penitence in you? Do not hide anything from me, but tell me exactly what your problems are, and I, for my part, will search out those remedies that will best meet your condition. For the fornicator needs one course of treatment, and the murderer another, and the dealer in magic charms another, while the materialistic man requires quite a different sort of help.'

The young man brought up groans from the depths of his heart and beat upon his breast, overcome with hysterical weeping. So complete was the confusion of his heart that he could not utter one articulate word.

When I saw him so devastated by a grief that deprived him of thought and speech, to such an extent that he was completely unable to explain to me what was the cause of his problems, I said to him, 'Calm yourself a little, my son, and control those wild thoughts of yours, and then tell me the whole matter, for Christ our God is well able to supply you with the help you need. After all, it was because of his boundless love for the human race and his unconditional mercies that he suffered all he suffered. It was all for our salvation. That was why he ate with the tax-collectors and never turned his face away from the prostitute, and welcomed the thief—that was how he earned this title, *the friend of sinners*. Last of all, he accepted the cross, and even so he will also accept you into his own arms with tears of joy when you repent and turn back to him. He never wants the death of a sinner; he wants him to return and live.'

Then, with a great effort, he choked back his tears and told me all.

'Reverend father, I am full up with all manner of crimes, a blot on the heavens above, and a blot on the earth. Two days ago I heard that the daughter of one of our leading men in this city had died; she was only a girl. She had been buried, dressed in magnificent clothes in a cemetery outside the city.

'Now I had for long enough been heavily involved in that accursed occupation [of grave robbing], and as soon as I heard this news, I went that very night to the grave and began to undress her. I stripped her of all she had on. I never even left her underwear, but took that away as well, leaving her as naked as the day she was born.

'Just as I was leaving the tomb, the girl sat up in front of me. She reached out with her left hand and grabbed my right hand. "Honestly now, my friend, was it really necessary for you to strip me naked? Do you have no respect for God? Do you have no fear of a future sentence of retribution? Should you not show compassion on a corpse such as I am? Are you completely unmoved by our shared humanity? Do you, a Christian, think it right to send me to stand before Christ naked? Have you no respect for my sex, even though it is the same sex that gave you life? Would you insult your own mother by the insults you have offered me? What defence, you wretched specimen of masculinity, can you possibly offer before the dreadful judgement seat of Christ for what you have done to me? While I was alive no strange man ever saw my face, but now, after my death, you strip my corpse and feast your eyes on my naked body. To what depths has our human condition sunk? Is this the heart, are these the hands, with which you will draw near and take the precious body and blood of our Lord Jesus Christ?"

'At such words and such sights, I began to shake uncontrollably, full of terror and alarm.

'"Let me go," I said, "I will never do such a thing again." But she replied, "You came in here of your own free will but don't imagine that you will go out just when you please. This place will serve as a common grave for the two of us. Nor think that you will die suddenly. There will be many a long day of suffering before you in utter misery give up your utterly miserable life."

'With tears I begged her to release me. I swore again and again by the Lord God, the Ruler of all, that never again would I have anything to do with this accursed occupation.

'Then after long supplication and an ocean of tears, she answered me, "If you wish to save your life and find deliverance from this heinous crime, you must give me your word that not only will you have nothing more to do with this despicable and disgusting trade, but that you will also at once and immediately renounce the world and become a monk, so as to repent of the evil you have done and live as a servant of Christ."

'I swore at once, "Not only will I do all that you have said, but on this very day without even returning to my home, I will go straight from here to the monastery."

'Then the girl ordered, "Dress me as you found me."

'When I had done so, she lay down again and died. Immediately, then, this wretched sinner left the cemetery and came straight here.'

When I had heard the young man's story, I applied to his case some healing words about fasting and repenting, and in due time I gave him the tonsure and clothed him in the holy habit of a monk. Later on I enclosed him in a cave to live as an anchorite in the city here. And here he is, daily giving thanks to God, and struggling mightily to find the true life.

Then there is the case of the sensible village woman, the daughter of a farmer, who was able to instruct the monk on the real meaning of chastity and restraint:

A Most Sensible Girl (39)

When we arrived at Antioch the Great, I heard from one of the priests of the church there this tale which he had had of the patriarch Anastasius.

There was once a monk from the monastery of the Abbot Severianus who was sent on a mission to the district around Eleutheropolis. While he was there, he put up at the house of a local farmer, a very devout man who had only one daughter, the mother having died some time before.

After the monk had been staying some days in the farmer's house, the devil, who will never leave a man in peace, stirred up foul longings in the brother's heart. He was in turmoil over this girl and was ever looking for a chance to jump her.

Then the same devil, who was the source of this inner strife, also provided him with the opportunity. The girl's father went off to Ascalon to fetch some things he needed, and this brother realized that the house was empty except for him and the girl. He approached her, intent on rape.

When the girl saw what a state he was in, all ablaze with passion and desire, she said to him, 'Calm down, calm down, don't do anything reckless here. My father won't be back today, nor tomorrow, so there is time for us to chat, and after that, the Lord knows, I will be more than eager to do whatever you desire.'

Then she began to spin these webs around him: 'Reverend father, how long have you been in your monastery?

'Seventeen years.'

And again she asked, 'Have you ever had a woman?'

'No.'

To which she replied, 'And is it your intention to destroy, in a single hour, all the fruits of your labours? Think how many tears you have shed in the effort to present your body, free of all stain, before Christ. But now, for the fleeting pleasure of a single hour, are you willing to suffer the loss of all that you have striven for so far? Then think too of this: if I give way to you, and you fall into sin with me, have you got a home ready for me? Can you provide for me?'

And the brother said, 'No.

Then the girl's response was, 'To speak the truth, for I tell no lies, if you humiliate me you are going to bring about enormous troubles.'

And the monk asked, 'What troubles?'

'Number one, you will have destroyed your very life. Number two, my life will be required of you, for you can rest well assured of this, and I affirm it to you under oath by him who said, "Do not deceive yourself" (I Cor. 3: 18). If you humiliate me, I will hang myself and you will then be charged with murder, and as a murderer you will be condemned in the court. So, no, before you let loose such grave disasters, run back at once to your monastery where you have such ample opportunity to pray for me.'

By then the monk had come to his senses and in all sobriety he departed from that farmer's house and returned to his monastery. There, bowing low before the abbot, he requested that he never again be sent outside the monastery.

Only three months later he departed to be with the Lord.

THE OLD RELIGION

Even at this late date the ruined temples of the old gods were still dotted about the landscape, mostly as the unseen backdrop of daily life and struggles. But sometimes they still played a vital role, as in the case of the man condemned to crucifixion:

Last Minute Reprieve (72)

Father Palladios once told us about a certain old man at his place who had been arrested for murder, and under torture—for this is the custom in Alexandria—he revealed that someone else had been his accomplice in the murder. The person he implicated was a young chap, only twenty years old.

While they were both being subjected to a heavy beating, the old man said, 'You were with me when I committed the murder.'

But the young man maintained, 'I had no part in the murder; I was nowhere near you.'

After some lengthy beatings, they were both sentenced to crucifixion, and were led out to the Fifth Mile, for that was where such sentences were usually carried out, near the spot where there is a derelict temple of Chronos.

When they arrived at the spot, the soldiers and the crowd decided to crucify the young man first. Then he, bowing low to the soldiers, begged them, 'For the Lord's sake, do me this one last favour, hang me up facing the sunrise so that I may keep my eyes fixed on that direction as I hang there.'

The soldiers' response was: 'What's this all about?'

To which he replied, 'Sirs, poor wretch that I am, it is only seven months since I received holy Baptism and became a Christian.'

At this the soldiers were very moved, almost to tears.

But then the old man in a vile temper shouted, 'By Serapis, you can hang *me* facing towards Chronos!'

Disgusted by such blasphemy, the soldiers left the young man and crucified the old man first. But while they were still hanging him up, a man, sent by the mayor galloped up on horseback, and shouted to the soldiers, 'Don't kill the young one. Bring him in.'

Not everyone found the new approach of the Christian preachers to their liking, and were cautious in their reactions:

The Convert (195)

While we were in Alexandria, Leontios, a devout and loyal follower of Christ, turned up from Pentapolis. He had been a resident of Cyrene for some years. This was in the days of the reverend father Eulogius, the pope of Alexandria, the one who later became bishop of Cyrene.

We were all together one day, chatting with one another, when Leontios told us that in the days when Theophilus had been the pope of Alexandria, the bishop of Cyrene was the professor Synesios. When this man had arrived in Cyrene, he came across an old friend of his, professor Evagrius by name. They had long been close and steadfast friends, since the days when they had been in the same school together.

However, this Evagrius was still an enthusiastic supporter of the old religion and the worship of idols. Bishop Synesios wanted very much to win the man over. He did more than want it; he worked for it and went through untold toils and trouble because of the love he had for this man from former days. However, the man would not budge; he utterly refused to listen to any of this new teaching. But the bishop, because of the sincere friendship he still had for the man, was absolutely fearless, and never ceased even for a day to teach, exhort and admonish him to put his faith in Christ and thus be recognized by him.

It happened one day that the professor advanced this argument to the bishop. 'My Lord Bishop, amongst all the things that I cannot accept there is this one especially. The Christians keep on talking about the end of this world, which they say is soon coming, and they say that after the end the whole human race from ages past will rise again, each in his body, a body which will be incorruptible and indestructible, so that they will live forever. And at that time everyone will receive his due recompense. The one who by gifts to the poor loaned his money to God, and the one who scattered his income liberally amongst the poor and needy will, in that new age in the heavens, receive from Christ a hundredfold greater treasure along with the gift of eternal life. Well, all that sort of argument sounds in my ears like a complete nonsense, a trick, and a joke.' But bishop Synesios asserted still more firmly that the whole Christian business was true, without a whiff of falseness within it, and he tried to prove that this was so with all kinds of sophisticated arguments.

After a very long time he did in fact persuade the man to become a Christian, and baptized him along with his children and his whole household. A little while after his baptism, he gave the bishop three hundred pounds of gold to be used for the poor, with these words, 'Accept this gold; use it for the poor and let me have a receipt, so that Christ will make it good when I come into his kingdom.' Synesios happily received the money and gave him the receipt he had asked for.

The professor lived for quite a few years after receiving holy baptism and then contracted a fatal illness. As he was on the point of death, he said to his children, 'If you care for me, place this document in my hands and bury me with it.' After his death they did everything just as he had requested and at his funeral placed the autographed copy of the receipt in his grave.

Then, the third night after the funeral, he appeared in a dream to bishop Synesios in his sleep. 'Come to the grave where I lie buried and take back that receipt which you signed. The debt has been repaid, more than repaid, and there is no more business outstanding between us. To give the proof for all this I have added my own signature to the document.' Up to that point, the bishop had been completely unaware that his signed receipt had been buried with the professor.

First thing in the morning he sent for the man's sons and asked them, 'What did you place in the grave along with your father?'

They assumed that he meant 'what money' and so they answered, 'Master, we placed nothing there apart from his shroud.'

'Think again. Did you not bury some document with him?'

When they realized that he was talking about a legal document, they brought out the whole story. 'O yes, Master, as he was dying he gave us a certain receipt with instructions that at his burial this document was to be given to him to hold in his hands, and no one was to know anything about it at all.'

Then the bishop told them about his dream of the previous night. He took the sons, along with some of the clergy and some of the leading men of the city, and together they went to the professor's grave. When they opened the grave they found the professor lying there, holding in his own hands the bishop's signed receipt, and when they took the receipt from his hands and opened it, they found fresh writing there in the professor's hand.

The addition ran thus: 'I, Evagrius the professor, send my greetings to Synesios the bishop. I have received now full payment and even more for the amount written in the receipt, and I have no further claim against you for the money which I gave to you and, through you, to Christ our God and Saviour.'

Those who read it were astounded, and for a long time could only stand there repeating, 'Lord have mercy,' and giving the glory to God who works such miracles and brings such reassurance to his servants.

The same Master Leontios confirmed the truth of this story, for he had preserved the signed receipt with the added signature of the professor up until this very day, and it is still stored in the treasury of the church at Cyrene. Whoever is given the office of treasurer there, along with the sacred vessels, receives this document and guards it with the utmost care so that he may pass it on safe and unharmed to his successors.

But, amidst the heresies, the pirates, the prostitutes and the bishops, there were still found many good priests who, unobserved and unthanked, pursued their duties and served God's people:

The Virtuous Priest (108)

When we were on the island of Samos, we visited that monastery called 'The Gracious Welcome'. Its abbot, Isidorus, was a very distinguished man, overflowing with love for everyone, straightforward and humble. Sometime later he became the bishop of the city of Samos. This was his tale:

About eight miles from town there is an estate on which there is a church. They had a wonderful priest there whose parents had forced him early on into a marriage against his own wishes. And though he was then a young man, and joined to his lawfully wedded wife, he was never seduced by the allurements of the flesh; he even persuaded his wife to live with him in complete chastity. The two learned the psalms off by heart, and together they would sing the Psalter in the church. Thus they both preserved their virginity even into old age.

It happened that one day this priest was brought before the bishop on a false accusation. The bishop, ignorant of the true state of affairs in the case, sent for the priest. He then proceeded to remove him from his charge, and relegated him to the lock-up where fallen clergy were customarily enclosed under close supervision.

While he was in prison, Sunday came around, and on the Saturday night a very good-looking young man appeared standing before him. 'Father, it's time to get up, get back to your church, so that you will be there to offer the holy oblation.'

The priest replied, 'I cannot, as long as I am locked up here.'

But the one who appeared told him, 'I will open the gate for you. Come on, follow me.' And undoing the prison door he first went through himself and then led out the priest and took him to within a mile of the village.

At daybreak, the one in charge of the prison discovered his absence and immediately reported it to the bishop in these words, 'The man has stolen my key and run off.'

The bishop agreed that he had indeed probably run away, and so he sent for one of his household lackeys and said, 'Go see if this priest is back in his village. But if he is, do nothing for the time being.'

The servant ran off and indeed found the priest in his church offering up the holy oblation. He returned to tell the bishop, 'He is there all right, and has already begun the liturgy.'

The bishop was now even more enraged against the man, and swore an oath that the next day he would lay on him the heaviest of punishments.

On the Sunday night, the lad who had previously appeared to the priest came to him again, 'Come on, let's go back to the spot in town the bishop has prepared for you.' So he took him and led him back and left him once more inside the prison, though the guard remained completely unaware.

Early on the Monday morning, the bishop learned from the guard that the priest was back in his place in the prison, but how he had got there the guard had no idea.

The bishop then sent for the priest and questioned him, 'How did you get out of prison? How did you get back in again without the guard knowing it?'

And he replied, 'There was a good-looking young man in splendid robes who said he was a servant of the bishop; he opened the gate for me and, contrary to justice, led me to within a mile of my village. Then last night he came and led me back.'

The bishop then lined up every servant in his household, but the priest could identify none of them. Then the bishop realized at last that it must have been an angel who had done this, so that the true worth of the priest should no longer be concealed, but should be recognized by all, and so that everyone could give glory to God who gives glory to those who serve him.

The bishop was greatly edified by the whole affair and sent the priest home, while dismissing his accusers with some very harsh words.

And here is another case of clerical virtue:

Mass on Time! (27)

About ten miles from the city of Aegina in Cilicia, there is a small village called Mardardos, containing a church dedicated to John the Baptist. The priest of the church was a great man, an old man far advanced in holiness.

One day the local people brought a case against him before the bishop of Aegina. 'Remove this old man from us,' they said, 'he is giving us a load of trouble.'

When the bishop asked what the charge was against him, they reported, 'On Sunday he will celebrate the liturgy one day at 9:00 a.m. and on the next at 3:00 p.m. Nor does he always celebrate it the way we have always had it.'

So the bishop took the old priest to one side and questioned him privately. 'My dear father, what is all this fuss about? You have no need to be instructed on the customs and canons of our holy church.'

To which the priest's answer was, 'You are absolutely in the right, my Lord, everything you say is correct and very clearly put; but I just don't know what to do next. When I have completed the vigil service for the feast of the Lord's Day, I always sit in my place next to the holy altar. Only when I see the Holy Spirit has come amongst us, only then do I begin the liturgy.'

When the bishop heard this he was amazed at the spiritual power of the man, so he went and calmed the villagers down, and sent them home in peace praising God as they went.

Such a man was appreciated, even if he wasn't completely up-to-date with the latest theological gambits:

A Theological Innocent (199)

One of the brothers told us about an old father who was very sincere, very holy, who regularly saw two angels standing one on his right hand and one on his left whenever he celebrated the Eucharist. Unfortunately however, this man had received his consecration from the heretics. But, being a theological innocent, he celebrated in all simplicity and guilelessness, not even aware he was doing anything wrong.

In the providence of God he was visited by a brother who was an experienced theologian. While he was there, the old man happened to celebrate the liturgy, and afterwards the brother (who was a deacon) said to him, 'Father, these words you are using at the liturgy do not belong to the orthodox faith. They are heretical.'

But the old man, on the strength of those angels he saw beside him at the liturgy, paid no heed to such words; he reckoned them nothing to them.

But the deacon persisted, 'My dear old chap, you are in the wrong. The church does not accept this form you are using.'

As the old father saw that he was being denounced and refuted by the deacon, he became aware of those familiar angels at his side, and so he asked them, 'This is what the deacon is saying about me. What do you say?'

And they told him, 'Relax! He is in the right.'

So the old man said to them, 'Then why didn't you tell me this?'

And their answer was, 'Because this is the way God has arranged things, so that people are set right by other people.'

From that day onwards the old father did everything in the proper way, and gave thanks to God and to that brother.

And with this small bouquet from the pastures of the Spirit we will have to be content today.